ALONE:

A WAY OF LIFE

A Short Story

DAVID LEE HENLEY

Dedication To Susan Henley

The Love Of My Life

Like the stars, life and the heavens have their seasons,   and our love endures through it all.

David Lee Henley

Preface

As we all wonder at times how it would be if we could take a break from our lives and get away from the monotony and drudgery of our lives even for a little while to seek the solitude of nothingness, we could not fathom the notion of doing it for a lifetime.

 The sheer boredom of having no communication or contact with others is what drives most to seek out a popular spot where everyone gathers.

Not that individuals require close and constant interaction with someone, but they do need to have a connection with the society at large, a desire to belong. A compulsion to connect is far stronger than any thought of self-imposed isolation.

 Isolation from the group has been used as a punishment since the dawn of time. To be ostracized from the group is an unthinkable punishment.

It is this awareness of our behavior that has prompted this short story. To delve into the life of one such individual that actually craves the isolation others shun. To see why one would want to live this lifestyle.

 We will listen to this individual's thinking and hopefully discover the answer and possibly understand why he somehow never received the same drive to belong as all the others around him, the construct of humans that links us all into the same blueprint of need and companionship.

Or maybe we will simply find that he just never wanted to belong.

Introduction

This short story starts with a monolog from the main character describing his own view of life as he has lived it. He is convinced he does not need nor want any connection to or even have any desire to be associated with humanity in general or at large.

That is a tough thing to do as the world is filled with people. So, he finds solace in getting away for short periods of time in an isolated environment where he can live his desire to be alone.

He finds though that even in a far-removed location, it is never quite far enough. There will always be some who will discover him, and whether he likes it or not, draw him into their conflicts.

This time it will force him to deal with the ramifications of their intrusion. It will cause him to disregard his own wants and needs for his self-appointed obligation of helping to return the intruding couple back to civilization.

It is strange that a man who wants nothing to do with people is thrust into such a predicament.

They do not make his mission to help easy at all. There is a constant threat to his life and theirs, the whole way back.

ALONE: *A WAY OF LIFE*

By: David Lee Henley

Since my earliest recollections as a child, I have never felt the companionship others seemed to enjoy. It has always eluded me in my interactions with family and friends.

Even while surrounded by a multitude of people, there was never that feeling of belonging or acceptance expected from these encounters.

In retrospect, I have to admit I never really put myself out there as one probably should have, and there was never a desire to do so.

So, here I am out here now, living my life as one separated from everything. Absorbing and partaking of all that is around me, which does not belong to the societal construct, and finally finding my peace, my wish to be alone is satisfied.

I have realized in retrospect; I was meant to be this way. My true happiness is within myself. My inner thoughts are all I have ever needed in the form of communication with the world around me.

Imbibing of the waters from the stream, eating the labors of my hunt. Caring only for myself, seeking only to be alone.

I suppose I was born too late. I would be better suited to have been born during the mountain man days when men sought to go alone into the wilderness and create a life along-side nature.

I looked at the wall calendar and said to myself; I guess I should go home now. The time I allotted myself to dream my fantasy of getting away from the world and being all alone is over.

A couple of days walk, and it would be back to the grind. The never-ending, never free, always busy doing something, grind.

While walking out of my self-imposed isolation from the outside world, I decided to stop at the waterfall one last time. It had always been my favorite spot to sit and reflect on life's little joke on me.

My purpose for being and lack of fulfilling any predetermined destiny was an enigma. It posed a combination of a challenge and a mystery.

What if anything at all was I to do about myself, and if I were to decide to change, how could I? It was incomprehensible to me that I would have a desire to change nor a will to do it at all. As I stated earlier, I have no aspiration to be a popular or famous person as everyone else thinks I should be.

Then breaking into my thoughts and self-analysis, I hear a scream. It was coming from the top of the falls.

As I was at the bottom near the actual cascading water, I could not see up to where the yelling was happening.

Then I heard clearly a woman yelling," no stop, get away from me."

Then I heard a man scream back at her. "I will have my freedom one way or another. You're making me do this!"

Then another scream from the woman and I saw her then as she was falling from the top of the cliff. She kept screamed as she fell. I saw her hit the water at a bad angle and knew she was in big trouble. Not just from the unseen man at the top of the cliff but by the way she hit the water. That would be bad.

I waited for her to come back up, but after not seeing her for a few seconds, I knew she was going to drown if she had not already.

I pulled off my shoes and jumped in. I swam to where I thought the current would have taken her, and sure enough there she was. I pulled her as fast as I could back to shore and seeing she was not breathing. I did all the steps I knew about drowning victims on her.

Let's see now how did that go?

First, check for breathing. Nope, not breathing. Check for pulse. No, no pulse either. Start compressions on the chest on top of the breastbone. Compress two inches at a rate of 100 to 120 pushes per minute.

Let's see, now what else. Com on man think. Oh, yea. Do thirty compressions and then two quick breaths into the mouth while holding her nose closed with her head tilted back.

Two breaths and thirty compressions. Two breaths and thirty compressions.

I kept doing that, for it seemed an eternity until she coughed and spat up water. She choked for a while but finally got control and looked up at me and quickly looked around.

I told her the man is not here.

She seemed to relax a bit visibly.

She looked at me then, probably a million questions going through her mind.

I said, "I heard you and the man, whoever he is, yelling, and then you fell into the water. I got you out and did CPR on you. That's all I know about this. If you don't want to talk about it, that's fine with me."

I was hoping she would not. I wanted nothing to do with any of this.

I don't know why I even jumped in and rescued her. I had never done anything like this for anyone ever before. I just stayed as distant as I could.

I did it without thinking, I told myself. So, what prompted me to do it? I had no ready patent answer.

She finally said, "thank you for saving me."

That was it. Nothing more. She obviously didn't want to talk about anything that went on between herself and the man.

She said, "how do I get to a phone from here?"

I said, "well, I am assuming you won't have a car as I am pretty sure your friend would have taken that. And he didn't come down to look for you, so I figure he thinks you are dead.

She looked happy about that.

"Good, maybe I can get out of here safely, "she said with doubt lingering in her voice.

I added, "we are in the middle of nowhere out here. The nearest phone is days away walking. I hiked in myself, so there is no easy way out."

"Oh, that is just great," she said with disgust."

She started to stand and yelled, "OHH."

Falling back down, she grabbed her ankle. "That hurts," she gasped.

I looked at her ankle, and sure enough, it was swelling and turning color.

"It looks like you sprained or broke your ankle," I said.

She said, "damn, just what I need right now!"

I thought to myself, ditto for me too, lady.

We both sat there for a few more minutes, both realizing she was still helpless. I, knowing I was not through helping her unless I just abandoned her, and she not wanting to impose any farther on me, but knowing she had no choice was waiting for me to offer it.

I said, "I have a cabin just over the rise over there. I will carry you to it if you wish. There is no way you can walk on that leg. We can wrap your ankle and try to keep the swelling down and work on it there, okay?"

She looked at me as if deciding if I was a threat or not and decided her position was not a good one and had no choice anyway in accepting my help.

She said, "I hate to be a bother to you, but it looks like I have no choice. I thank you again."

I stood and helped her up. I let her climb on my back with her arms over the top of my shoulders and her legs wrapped around my waist, so carrying her would be much more comfortable, and took her to my cabin. She was not as heavy as I thought she would be.

I was aware when we finally made it and were inside the cabin, that we were both soaking wet.

I told her, "look, I am not trying to be weird, but we need to get out of these wet clothes. I have some spare clothes you can wear until yours are dry. I can give them to you, and you can change them in the bathroom over there."

She looked at me with apprehension.

I said, "if I wanted to do something to you here, you couldn't stop me, I said bluntly and slightly insulted. Do whatever you want. But when we wrap that ankle, you won't be able to get out of those pants you're in now."

She knew that was all true.

"I'm sorry, and I apologize. Yes, I could use some dry clothes. Thank you once again," she said.

I brought her a change of clothes and helped her to the bathroom where she changed. I could hear her as she worked the pants down over the swollen ankle. "OH, augh, damn."

Finally, she opened the door dressed in my clothing, oversized for her as it obviously hung on her frame.

I helped her to the couch and tended to her ankle. I first took a large cooking pot I had and filled it with cold water. It was the best I could do in lieu of having no ice handy.

Then after twenty minutes in the water, I wrapped her ankle in the prescribed manner I had taught myself, as a just in case I got myself into this same situation.

Starting with a point farthest from the heart, I wrapped it not to tightly and had her elevate the foot by lying on the couch with her foot above her heart. I gave her some aspirin for the pain.

Every three hours, I re-soaked her foot to try and help bring the swelling down. While she was resting, I went out and found a branch and cut her a staff to use to help when she needed to get around. It would keep her weight off of her foot and help with balance.

I suddenly became aware I was not alone. It is a feeling you get when you are tuned into your surroundings as keenly as I was. It had saved me on more than one occasion with wild animals.

I take such warnings very seriously. I could not see or hear anything, but I knew something was out there. The hair on the back of my neck was standing up, a good sign of danger from the subconscious mind.

I pretended not to notice and went about doing my chore with the staff, and when I was finished, I went back to the cabin.

I had another chore to do. And it would be done before nightfall. I had an unannounced visitor that did not want to be found out at the moment. That told me it was probably the man from earlier. I was not going to be a victim for anyone for any reason.

Whatever these two people had between them was not my concern. My only interest was what the man intended to do next? He was not acting as a reasonable person would, who had witnessed his lady friend going over a cliff.

 He had not found his way down to show even the slightest worry over her well-being, nor did he come and introduce himself and attempt to help in this crisis. He was going to be a problem.

Well, he was not the only one that could be a problem.

I gave the lady the staff, and she was very grateful.

 She said, "it will come in handy in helping me to get around."

She said, "you are a strange man. I have been here all day and not once have you wondered about me, or the situation I find myself in, not even my name."

I said, "it is none of my business.

"If you had wanted to tell me, I figured you would do so, being nosy is the least of my faults."

I guess she was getting bored, and as most women are, they need to talk. So, she started by asking me about myself.

"So, are you a hunter? I see you have a lot of heads of animals all around, so I suppose that was a dumb question," she corrected herself.

I didn't answer as she had already fielded the response.

I watched her mull over things in her mind. I knew then she was going to tell me about her friend.

She finally decided to talk. "I think you deserve an explanation for what went on earlier.

"By the way, my name is Jill, and my husband is Jack, and yes, I know that is a strange combination for obvious fairytale reasons, she added wanting to get the old clichés out of the way.

"I caught my husband, Jack, with another woman, and he has apparently chosen to divorce me. I didn't want that; I wanted to work things out. It seems, very plainly to me now, I should have gone that route myself.

"He brought me to this location where it is evident; he planned to kill me. I figured that out as he pushed me off the cliff into the water to drown.

"If not for you, he could have claimed it was an accident. But now it is attempted murder.

"He is a very dangerous man. If he knew I was still alive, it would be bad for both of us; I am certain of that."

I looked at her.

"Lady, I said, I think you still have a problem. I am almost sure your husband is lurking around out there somewhere, just waiting to get to you."

She was petrified. "What did you say? Is Jack out there now? How do you know that?"

"Just a feeling I have, I'm not wrong, usually," I remarked.

"What can I do, she cried out? He will want to keep me from telling on him, and you're in danger also as a witness."

"I said, well, this is a problem. I can't kill him because you have stated you wanted to get back together with him. I guess the only thing I can do is detain him. Or at least try. I never captured a human before in this way. It sounds like fun."

She looked at me with a puzzled look. She was wondering who was the real crazy man now.

I began to think, and then, to build my trap.

Late that evening, I made a point to get plenty of wood for the fireplace and let whoever was out there get the feeling I was unaware of him. I settled in and began the waiting game.

At around eight, I shut off the lights and pretended to go to sleep.

At ten, I heard the door. It was opening, and someone was coming in. I waited till he was at the right spot and released my trap.

"Son-of-a-bitch," he yelled.

I lit the lantern and got a view of the man finally.

I walked over and saw his knife.

I said, "let go of the blade, or I will use this spear on you."

He settled down as he saw the spear at his throat. He let go of his knife. This guy had meant to do some real damage. I was tempted to finish this now, but now I had a witness, and I was not willing to kill her too.

Instead, I turned the pointy end of the spear around and hit the man in the head with the blunt round brass ball on the other side. He went limp. I needed to get him out of the netting that had wrapped around him when the trap was released. It was somewhat amusing the way I had set it up.

When he had walked under the location where I had planned him to be, I released the string that was holding the netting up on rings on the ceiling.

 That allowed the net to fall straight down and cover the man. As he couldn't see anything, he thrashed about and got himself even more caught in the netting until he fell. That was when I lit the lantern.

 His wife was frozen in fear looking at him.

"Is he dead? Did you kill him," she asked?

"Do you care," I countered?

She didn't answer?

That probably made her question herself as to her own agenda for the man called Jack.

I took the opportunity to put a pair of handcuffs on him. Out here in the wild, you never know what might happen, and I always believed in being prepared. So, I had a couple of pairs of cuffs as a just in case. It looks like I was right; life follows you everywhere.

I told the lady, "you can watch him if you want, but I am getting some sleep. It has been a long day."

She said, "what am I supposed to do if he tries something?"

I said, "whatever you want to. Or just yell. Whatever works for you. I personally don't like killers, so whatever you do makes no difference to me. You do know what, whatever means, right? Goodnight."

I put a chain around the cuffs and locked the chain to a floor bolt with a ring, and went to sleep in the corner chair. He was not harming anyone tonight.

The next morning, I woke up and saw the man had sat up and was looking at the lady with a hate as big as Texas in his eyes. She was still asleep and didn't see it. Probably for the best. He saw me stirring and refocused his hate-filled eyes on me.

"I owe you one mister," he said with a deadly tone.

I said, "oh, you talking to me."

I walked over and kicked him in the face.

He flew backward and yelled, "damn you."

I picked him up and said, "say you are sorry right now, or I am going to gut you."

He looked at me with a whole new respect.

He said, "ok, I am sorry," then stupidly added, "for now."

So, he was still not getting it.

I hit him again.

"No respect, I said. Now let's try it again. Say you are sorry."

He was getting the idea finally how this was going to play out.

He said, slowly and deliberately, "I'm sorry."

I said, "bright boy. You come inside my house to do me and my guest harm, and you think I should care how or what you think? You really need to stop and ask yourself, why would a guy want to live out here in the middle of nowhere all alone?

"Maybe I have issues, and you shouldn't push my buttons too hard, eh?"

He began to see that he was not the only hard-ass around these parts.

"So, what now," he asked?

I answered, "I haven't thought that far ahead yet. That depends on what you two work out. I know I will not just let you go with your attitude. I won't be spending my life looking over my shoulder for some ass looking for payback. Remember, you started this party."

Jack said, "what do you mean it depends on what Jill and I work out."

I said, "well you tried to kill her yesterday, and by the way, you actually did kill her, I just brought her back with some CPR. You can thank me anytime you want. No? I didn't think so."

"So, Jill," I said, "we're all stuck here until you get well enough to walk. So, what do you want to do?"

"I want to get out of here and get away from him," she said.

Jack said, "that is what I've been trying to do, you idiot, you just won't let me go. So, I did the only thing left to me. You did this to yourself."

Jill cried out, "how can you put this back on me? I loved you? I was willing to forgive you for cheating around on me. I never in a million years would have thought you hated me so much as to kill me. What sane man does that?

"You can have your divorce, and you can spend the rest of your life in jail for all I care."

"What do you mean, are going to turn me in," Jack said?

"You tried to kill me, what do you think," she said?

He got serious then. "Ok, if that is how you want it. Just know this, if I get the chance, I am going to finish it. So, your boyfriend over there better watch his back."

I stood up and walked over to Jake and kicked him in the face again. That sent him flying back and out again.

"You don't learn very fast," I mumbled.

I told Jill, "while he's sleeping it off, I am going hunting.

"We need some food if we're are staying here for a while longer. Be back later."

She said, "you're leaving me here alone with him?"

I said, "same as before, if he acts up, do what you need to do."

I was happy to get out of there. People and their relationship problems drag me down.

 I didn't know who wanted who to leave more. It seemed like a stalemate all around.

I could see why he wanted out of the marriage. The lady sure liked pushing his buttons. But his cheating didn't help matters much. Everyone has their faults.

I shot a deer, cleaned and skinned it, and brought back the meat for processing. I saw the killer and his wife were still at it. So, I just took the deer meat to my cleaning and cutting table and cut the deer meat up for use. I started a slow, low fire in the smoker shack and began turning the venison to jerky for more extended storage and use.

By the time I got back to the house, they were taking a break from the constant bickering and threats. Good, I didn't want to have to listen to all that.

"So, your jaws getting tired," I quipped.

The man said, "are you going to starve us, or do we get some food around here?"

I said, "we, you said, we? You mean you're thinking of her needs again? Well, well, that is progress."

Jack said, "that's not what I meant."

"So, Jill, do you like deer meat?"

Jill stated with horror, "you killed a deer?"

"That is what is running around out there unless you want me to bring you a bear," I said.

She said," I never had deer meat. I don't know if I can eat that!"

"Well, suit yourself," I said.

I got the fire in the cookstove going and started cooking a few deer steaks. The aroma permeated the cabin, and everyone smelled it and made them all hungrier. I knew neither had eaten for a full day or longer, so they had to be practically starving.

I put a plate of steaks on the table and said. "Pardon me, but I am hungry, and these steaks are getting cold."

I cut a bite and chewed it groaning aloud, "oh man, is that good."

The girl looked at it and finally said, "I guess I could try it."

I said, "help yourself."

She hobbled over and sat down. She took a cut from a steak and put it in her mouth.

"Oh, that is good, she said surprised, it tastes different from beef, but it is good." She continued to eat.

Jack said, "what about me?"

I said, "say, please!"

Jack knew if he were going to be fed, he would have to grovel, so be it.

He would have his chance sooner or later.

"Please, may I have some food," he asked, holding his acid tongue this time.

"Sure," I said, and tossed him a steak.

He caught it and said, "what about a knife and fork and plate."

I told him, "murderers don't get things to kill with, get used to it."

I could see the calculations in his head. He was figuring I would eventually make a mistake, and that would be it for me. He might have something there. I have to be sure of every move all the time, while I also only need to be wrong just once for him to kill me.

As the days slowly went by, I was feeling the pressure, and he knew it. The long walk out was going to be where he would make his play.

Jill had gotten to where she could stand on her foot again, and with the therapy I gave her, she was getting better fast. It would soon be time to go.

"So, Jack, I asked, where is the car? It would make everything a whole lot easier if we simply drove out."

He said, "I don't remember. I got lost following you here."

Well, I knew that was a lie. But there was nothing short of torture I was going to be able to do about it.

The next morning, I decided to try and find it. I went back to the waterfall and went along the trail that led up to the top of the falls and started looking around. Sure enough, there it was.

Good, I thought, this would make things much more manageable.

Well, I thought it would until I checked the car and found it was missing three plug wires.

Cautious man. I had a greater respect for him now. He was thorough. Yes, but two could play that game. I took three more plug wires and buried them as I am sure he did the same with the ones he took.

If it worked out that he won this little game we had going, he was going to be surprised when he tried using the car.

I also took the vehicle registration with his name on it so that when we left the cabin, I would leave a note with a message and his registration on the table telling of the happenings around here and if I didn't return to destroy the message then Jack had probably killed the lady and me.

In the next couple of days, I was busy getting the supplies ready for the trip. I put all the heavy things in the pack killer Jack was going to have to carry.

That would at least tired him out somewhat when time to make camp came around. I figured it to be a three-day trek with the lady still not up to one-hundred percent.

They had been doing a lot of talking to each other. It was like a family therapy counselor would try. Get them talking, and maybe they could work it out. The only problem was that pesky; he tried to kill her thing, still hanging in the air. That was a kind of deal-breaker in my book. But who knows, time will tell.

We took off the next morning. It was looking like good weather all the way, warm but not hot days, and not too cold nights. The couple walked side by side, talking and laughing, remembering the good times.

They seemed to be falling in love again all over again.

I, for my part, had my doubts. If I was Jack and time was running out, I would turn on the charm just like he was doing and try to convince her not to prosecute. To maybe even give it another try.

 Jack was even trying to buddy up to me, saying how sorry he was that he had acted so aggressively when he first came into the cabin. He sees things more clearly now. I played along.

Don't worry about it, I said. I don't have to live with you. Just get you out of here. I don't harbor any grudges. You got the worst of this deal as I see it anyway.

He looked at me then, and I could see he knew I wasn't buying his act one bit. So, he continued to work his magic on the lady.

I have to admit he sure knew how to charm the ladies. Jill was soaking it up. She looked like she was coming around to his side.

I might need to start keeping an eye on both of them.

That's the thanks I get. I save her life, and she helps the guy that tries to kill her take me out. Just wonderful.

So, once again, why do I like to be alone?

The first night was mostly peaceful. I wrapped and locked a chain around a tree and hooked killer Jack to it with the cuffs. Jill slept near him but not close enough that he could reach her. She wasn't that smitten just yet.

The jerky I had made was good. We all had some for our meal.

Morning came too soon, but it is what it is. I gave everyone some jerky to start the day. Jack was feeling the soreness from carrying the heavy pack all day but didn't complain. He wanted to show his good side at all times. Fine by me.

He saw I was not going to give him an opening to catch me off guard. His only option was his wife. He was stepping up his game on her.

Now he was talking about what-ifs. What if we could work this out! What if we could try again! He was starting to have deep feelings for her yet again. The baloney was getting cut thicker with each slice.

I saw what they didn't. A snake crossing just ahead of them. I always keep a watch for snakes. I hate snakes of any variety. Two-legged or no legs, they are all the same. If they can bite you, they will.

I pulled my pistol and ran up on the oblivious couple. Just as they were next to the snake, I could see it was rearing up to strike. The fools didn't even hear the hissing; they were so into each other.

Or were they. I had just enough time to see Jack stop with Jill right in line with the coming strike. He was keeping her occupied as best as he could. Jack was keeping her focus on him. Yea, he had seen the snake and was setting her up for the kill.

I shot just in time. I am a good shot if I do say so myself. I practice all the time. I took the snakes head clean off with the first shot. Jill screamed and looked at me. Jack just looked at me. His gaze had a different meaning. I had spoiled his little surprise for his wife. Well, that was just too bad, I say.

Jill yelled, "what the hell are you doing? Are you crazy?"

I said, "that is still up for debate. But as for why I shot, look down at your feet."

She looked, jumped back, and screamed again.

"Snake," she cried out.

I said, "calm down. It is dead. But, on the bright side, at least now we have something new for supper."

Jack, never wasting a moment to get in her good graces. Grabbed her in a hug and said, "oh honey, are you all right? That was a close one."

She ate it up. Jack cared about her; she no doubt was thinking. She hugged him back.

I thought she might be better off if I had let the snake bite her. Either way, she was a goner.

He looked at me from over her shoulder and smiled.

I just said, "well played."

Yes, the snake was a good change of pace. It was huge, and Jill wanted none of it.

"More for me," I said.

She ate the deer jerky.

We would be out of the forest tomorrow, so if killer Jack were going to try something, he would have to do it tonight. I stopped all of that nonsensical thinking.

I not only put cuffs on his hands; I also put chain on his legs and locked it tight. I basically hogtied him. I wanted a good night's sleep.

Jill slept next to him, so I got up and went into the woods and hid, just in case. I figure he had gotten to her, and this was not going to end well for her. But I was not going down with her.

People can be so gullible, so trusting, so stupid. Gullible in that, in their innocence and naivety, they become trusting in any streetwise smooth talker that comes along.

You can sometimes get them to see the truth with facts, but you can't fix stupid. That is why I don't bother to worry any longer about Jill. Some people are just born victims. They seek out or simply put themselves into the most unwise positions.

She knows without a doubt that her husband was trying to kill her. And with just a few words of endearment from him, she's ready to forgive him and allow him the opportunity to try again, believing he is a changed man until the moment he tosses her over the falls once again. Just stupid.

I have to admit, though; it is fascinating watching it all play out right in front of me.

When morning came, I went back to camp. There they were talking as if nothing had ever happened between them. Now I knew how this was going down.

I asked Jill to walk with me. I left Jack cuffed to the tree. When we were out of sight and ear-shot, I got to it.

"Okay, Jill, I said. You tell me what your decision is! I am not going to waste any more of my time in bringing your husband back if you are going to let him go with no charges. I might as well let him go right now, and you both can leave and do whatever you want.

"But in good conscience, I have to warn you; he will kill you at some time. He is a good con-artist, liar, and we both know him to be an attempted murderer. Whether you believe me or not, I am telling you he set you up for that snake to bite you, I saw it as plain as day.

"He will say and do anything to get you to change your mind about turning him in. And from what I see, he has done a bang-up job.

"So, what is your answer? I got things to do."

She looked at me for a minute and finally said, "you are probably right about him. He is a charmer. But I still love him. I know I am a fool, but I can't help myself. I can't explain it. I swore an oath when we were married, for better or worse till I died. Well, if that is what it comes to, then so be it.

"But I want to thank you for all you have done for me, even if it turns out to be for nothing.

"You are a good man. I don't think you give yourself enough credit in that regard. You saved me; you took care of me; you protected me on numerous occasions.

"I don't deserve all you have done for me with this stupid decision I am making, and yes, I know it is a foolish decision. But it is what it is, as they say.

"So, to answer your question, I am not going to turn him in."

I reached into my pocket and handed her the key to the cuffs.

"It's your life, lady, I said. Go ahead and enjoy it while you can. Just leave my stuff where it is, I'll be back later to get it. Follow the trail, and it will take you into town; if you make it."

I turned and walked away.

She watched me for a while. I am sure she had wanted to yell for me to come back but was unable to, probably because she had just convinced herself, or was it because she had trapped herself in her own bull story.

As an avid hunter, I was good at sneaking around unheard and undetected. As soon as I was out of her sight, I began to circle around in a wide ark and sneak up on the site where Jack was still cuffed to the tree.

She had made it back, and they were talking for a while longer. She definitely was having second thoughts now that she was all alone with Jack, or she would have simply turned him loose.

I am sure he wanted to know where I was, she would tell him I left, and she was deciding about his release.

She finally went over and uncuffed him from the tree. He was free and alone with her.

He looked around to be sure I was really gone, and he hugged and kissed her, smart boy, that one. Get her totally at ease for when he would do her in. Find another accident location.

They started down the trail then, hand in hand.

They walked for a long while; I knew he was making sure I was really gone before he made his move.

Then they came to a deep ravine. It had steep sides, the perfect place. Jack guided Jill over closer to the rim as they walked. I had to get nearer. She saw how close they were getting to the edge and stopped.

She looked at him, and they started talking. I couldn't hear yet, but as I crept closer, I was able to start picking up their conversation.

Jill said, Jack, "I told you I was not going to turn you in and prosecute you; why do you have to do this?"

Jack said, "I still want out, and I know you. You will never sign the divorce papers. This is still the best way. Till death do us part, right baby?

"I will tell them how horrible it was that you got to close to the edge and slipped. I didn't have time to get to you before you fell, such a tragic accident," Jack said, grinning at her.

He grabbed her then, and she began to fight for her life. She was screaming and thrashing. That was what I was waiting for, so he would not see nor hear me coming as he was now occupied with her.

I got to them both just as he was pushing her over. Damn, I was too late.

I grabbed him, so his push to get her over the cliff was not as strong as he had wanted or needed, but it was enough. She disappeared over the edge. Jack and I both went down to the ground together. Getting on our feet, Jack instantly began to fight me. We started swinging on each other.

This battle was close and personal for both of us. Jack finally knocked me down close to the edge, and as I was trying to get up, he lunged at me to try and shove me over the side. I dropped quickly, and as he passed by, he tripped on my foot. He stumbled, and not being able to stop himself went over the edge. I could hear him screaming all the way down.

 I quickly got up and went over to the place where Jill had gone over and saw she was hanging on to a ledge about seven feet down. It was a small thing, but it gave her just enough of something to hang on to for a short while. I could not reach her. She was already slipping, and her grip was precarious enough.

I glanced around and went to a tree nearby and broke off a limb. I raced back to the rim and guided the branch down to her. I said, Jill, you have to grab the branch, and I will pull you up. You can do it. Just grab the branch and hang on.

She yelled, I can't; I'm slipping.

I said if you want to live you have to do it.

She knew it was true; this time, she had to save herself.

It was as if she was having a life review. All the times she had let others come to her defense or to guide her life the way they thought it should be. An awakening within herself to finally take charge and be accountable for her own actions and destiny. I thought this was a pretty good time for her to finally get her act together.

She looked at the branch and up at me. Okay, she said, okay.

With that said, she concentrated on the motions she would have to do, and indecision vanished from her mind. She let go of her grip on the ledge with one hand and grabbed the branch.

Once she had one hand on each, she let go of the shelf with her other hand and was now gripping the branch with both hands.

I said, "good girl." I started pulling her up.

It seemed to take forever, but eventually, she came over the rim onto solid ground. Once she was on flat ground again, I let go of the branch and went to her, pulling her farther from the edge before I stopped and let her go.

I reached out and brought her into an embrace. She clung to me hard. I knew that would help settle her down. Maybe I needed a hug also, though I don't know why, I like being alone, right?

She broke down then as all the horror of the last few minutes came fully to her mind. After a long cry, she finally loosened her hold on me. I let go of her, and we both sat there looking at each other.

I knew she had a million things she wanted to say to me, but was too ashamed to say it. You could read it on her face.

I saved her the trouble or humiliation; however, you want to think of it.

"Now you're free, I said. Jack tripped as he was trying to push me over the cliff; he could not stop himself from going over the edge."

That pretty much said all that was necessary. Jill could never be sure it happened just that way, but accepted it as the truth.

I had a while to contemplate the last few days as we silently continued into town and was surprised at myself that I was looking at life a little differently than previous self-evaluations.

I was starting to care about what happened to the lady, to Jill. And not only her but the whole town. I was finally getting it.

A society needs membership to function. One could not solely be responsible for only oneself. It takes a group cooperative effort to make everything work together.

Maybe next year, when I take my vacation and seek the solitude nature provides, I might alter my policy of oneness and bring along a couple of people that have tried to be my friends and see how that works out. Who knows?

I guess Jill might not be the only one who can look inward and see a different light shining. A change in perspective.

Finally, in town, we went to the police station because we needed to inform the authorities of all that had happened.

As we went into the building, everyone said good morning, sir.

Jill looked at me but didn't say anything.

We continued forward until we came to the desk Sargent.

He was busy doing some paperwork, and without looking up, he said, "how may I help you?"

I said, "you can show the lady more respect, Sargent."

He looked up.

He saw who I was and said, "Sheriff, your back. We were getting worried about you. You're over a week overdue. How was your trip? Did you bring us some deer meat?"

I said, "that could wait, and no, I didn't. This lady has to make a statement about an incident that happened up on the ridge.

"You need to send a recovery team to the valley floor to recover the body of her husband. He fell off the cliff there."

That got the Sargent's attention.

 "Yes sir, and I am sorry for your loss Mam," the Sargent added.

The Sargent left to get things rolling.

Jill looked at me in total disbelief and said, "You're the Sheriff?"

I said, "guilty as charged. Then I added, it seems that is what everyone says."

BIOGRAPHY

David Henley, born in West Memphis, Arkansas, grew up while moving from place to place. He spent three years in Germany in the Army and has worked many jobs starting at age twelve. Such diversity has allowed a great deal of interaction with society and given him many encounters from which to draw life lessons from in his writings.

In his debut book {POEMS, LYRICS AND DIVERSE THOUGHTS}, he imparts a particular moment in time, that everyone can find within themselves which should awaken a memory they have at one time lived. The lyrics in this book are from the songs he has written.

{THE LAST RIDE IS FREE} is his first thriller fantasy novel about three people and their adventures in the world of criminals and honest society. A journey from the dark side of humanity toward more enlightened soul-searching encounters.

{THE LAST RIDE IS FREE: BOOK TWO} is his continuation of a fantasy thriller novel in a series about the Malone family. It is packed with the same nonstop action as the first book. It has also brought their son into the fold as an agent working alongside his parents, Mario and Julie.

{THE LAST RIDE IS FREE: BOOK THREE} is this finale novel in the series of the Malone Family. It brings the whole family full circle. As usual, it has many adventures and missions but also has secrets about the family that even they were not aware of all finally brought to fruition.

{A DAY IN THE LIFE OF SARGENT SMITH} is a short story about an unknown group of entities searching for what makes a common man different from all others. It is a fantasy action thriller looking into a subject long ignored.

Made in the USA
Middletown, DE
31 October 2024

63123235R00031